Ancestor Day

Remembering Family

Look at the **lanterns.**

We will see the lanterns.

Look at the food.

We will see the food.

Look at the **incense.**

We will see the incense.

Look at the red turtle cake.

We will see

the red turtle cake.

9

Look at the children.

We will see the children.

Look at the paper man.

We will see the paper man.

13

Look at the fire.

We will see the fire.

Glossary

incense

lanterns